The Palomino

Rachel Damon Criscione

The Rosen Publishing Group's
PowerKids Press™
New York

To Emily Criscione, the golden girl

Published in 2007 by The Rosen Publishing Group, Inc.
29 East 21st Street, New York, NY 10010

First Edition

Editors: Melissa Acevedo and Amelie von Zumbusch
Book Design/Layout: Ginny Chu
Illustrations: p. 6 Map by Greg Tucker

Photo Credits: Cover and title page, p. 12, Robert Maier/Animals Animals; pp. 4, 8 Photos courtesy of David R. Stoecklein; p. 7 Prado, Spain, Madrid, Giraudon;/Bridgeman Art Library; pp. 11, 15 © Bob Langrish; pp. 16, 19 © Kit Houghton/Corbis; p. 20 Photo and pedigree courtesy of Marleen Cowie.

Library of Congress Cataloging-in-Publication Data

Criscione, Rachel Damon
  The Palomino / Rachel Damon Criscione.— 1st ed.
      p. cm. — (The Library of horses)
  Includes bibliographical references and index.
  ISBN 1-4042-3449-7 (lib. bdg.)
  1. Palomino horse—Juvenile literature. I. Title.
  SF293.P3C75 2007
  636.1'3—dc22

                                    2005026678

Manufactured in the United States of America

Table of Contents

This picture shows a herd of horses in Nebraska. The palomino horse's golden color makes it stand out from the rest of the herd. This is just one reason these horses are so special!

4

The Golden Horse

It is easy to spot a palomino in a group of horses. Its golden coat and its silvery white mane and tail make it stand out from the crowd. Palomino is the color of a horse, not a **breed**. Quarter horses, Thoroughbreds, Morgans, Arabians, American saddlebreds, and Tennessee walking horses are all horse breeds that can also be **registered** as palominos.

The palomino horse has a colorful history. The golden horse was once the pride of Queen Isabella's Spanish court. Palominos were also trained by Native Americans in the Southwest. Today palominos can be seen in horse shows around the world.

A Horse with a History

Queen Isabella of Castile in Spain collected and **bred** horses at her home in Remuda Royal during the fifteenth century. She was proud of her horses and saw that they were well cared for. Since palominos were among the queen's favorites, she made sure that these horses were carefully bred.

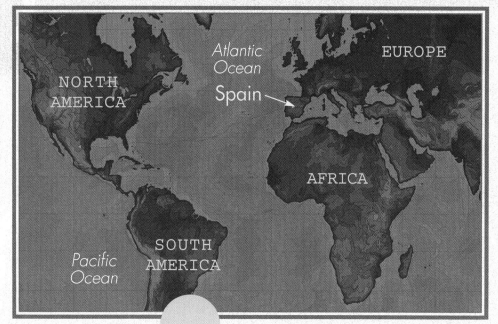

This map shows the path the explorers traveled from Spain to the New World.

Spanish explorers sailed to North America and South America in the 1500s to settle and claim land for Spain. These explorers brought palomino horses with them. Records show that palomino **stallions** and **mares** were brought to the land that is now Mexico. These

This painting of Queen Isabella of Castile was created during the fifteenth century. Castile is an area in northern Spain.

horses later bred with other horses that the Spanish brought to the American Southwest. It would be more than 200 years, however, before palominos were as carefully bred in America as Isabella's golden horses had been in Spain.

In addition to their golden color, palomino horses have white tails and manes. Can you spot the palominos in this picture?

Legend of the Palomino

A popular **legend** has it that the first palomino breeder in the United States was named Don Estaban. He was a wealthy farmer who lived in California in the 1800s. One year Don Estaban needed extra horses to work on his farm. He sent his workers into the hills to capture more horses. Don Estaban promised to give the person who brought him the most beautiful horse many pieces of silver.

A young Native American worker spotted a stallion with what looked like a golden coat underneath its thick coat of dust. After he washed the horse and brushed its mane, the boy presented the palomino horse to Estaban. This winning horse is said to be the first recorded American palomino.

Cremellos

One of the first things horse breeders in the United States learned about palominos was that they do not breed true to type. This means that a palomino stallion and a palomino mare have golden-colored **foals** only half of the time. When two golden palomino horses are bred, their foal may be a **cremello**. A cremello is a pale, cream-colored horse with blue eyes. Although cremellos' parents are palominos, cremellos do not meet the requirements to be registered with the Palomino Horse Breeders of America (PHBA). They may, however, be registered with the Palomino Horse Association.

Since palominos do not breed true to type, a palomino foal often has only one parent that is a palomino. The foal's other parent is usually a chestnut-colored horse. Chestnut horses have reddish gold coats, manes, and tails.

This cremello horse is running through a field.

Some palomino horses, such as the horse shown on the left, have a white strip across the front of their face. This sort of marking is called a stripe.

Not Every Gold Horse Is a Palomino

A palomino can be a horse of any breed. However, not every horse with a golden coat is a palomino. For a horse to be registered with the Palomino Horse Breeders of America, it must meet several requirements. The rules state that a palomino must have a coat the color of a United States gold coin, and a white mane and tail. White markings are allowed on the horse's face and below its knees.

A palomino is between 14 and 17 hands high, depending on the breed of the horse. Horses are always measured in hands. One hand is 4 inches (10 cm). The height of a horse is found by measuring the horse from its **withers**, the highest point on a horse's shoulders, to the ground.

Palominos Are All-around Horses

Palominos are not only valued for their beauty but also for the skills and strengths of the different horse breeds from which they come. The work palominos do best depends on their breed. For example, a palomino may be a quarter horse, a strong horse known for its speed when running short distances. A palomino can also be a Morgan horse. Morgan horses are known for their strength and ability to pull wagons.

Palominos are used to work with cattle on farms and as **recreational** horses. They take part in both English-style and Western-style horse shows. You can see palominos of many different breeds taking part in races at **rodeos**, playing in sporting events, and marching in parades.

Palomino horses have many uses. The cowboy in this picture is using his palomino horse to help him rope a cow.

Once a horse becomes used to carrying a rider, it can also be trained to do special tasks like jumping.

Training a Palomino

Training a palomino or any other horse requires a lot of time. A trainer starts working with a foal when it is just a few weeks old. At first the two just play, so the horse will get used to being around people. Slowly the young horse will start to wear a **saddle** and other things that will be used for riding.

A horse must get used to having weight on its back long before people start to ride it. First the horse learns to walk around with a heavy blanket on its back. More blankets are added as the horse gets used to the weight. Finally the horse is fitted for a saddle. When a palomino is about two years old, its body is usually strong enough to carry the weight of a rider.

You Cannot Judge a Horse by Its Color

Since the way a horse acts is based on its breed, not its color, not all palominos act the same way. Some are calm, and some are nervous. Some palominos are gentle, and others are forceful. Their conduct depends on their breed.

There are three basic types of palominos. These are **stock horses**, recreational horses, and parade horses. The quarter horse is a good example of a sturdy stock horse, or workhorse. The high-stepping American saddlebred is a favorite recreational horse for trail riding and horse show events. Each New Year's Day, palomino horses of many breeds walk in the Tournament of Roses Parade in Pasadena, California. The beautiful horses proudly prance down the street with a uniformed rider sitting high in the saddle.

This palomino horse is being led around at a horse show.

This is a pedigree of Im A True Blonde, a palomino quarter horse. Pedigrees trace the history and bloodlines of an individual horse. The picture below shows Im A True Blonde.

THE PALOMINO HORSE BREEDERS OF AMERICA, INC.

NAME   Im A True Blonde

REGISTRATION NUMBER   59708

FOALED DATE   1/12/91   STATE NY

SEX   Mare

BREEDER   45182 Marleen Cowie

Perry, NY

OWNER   45182 Marleen Cowie

Perry, NY

	Dun Played	Counterplay Q 265798
SIRE Palomino Jets Played First Q 1818986 P00043612	Q 1006688	Aledo Bar's Lady Q 168881
	Miss Jet Away Q 973041	Jetaway Reed Q 336518
		Keet Q 233773
	Blondy's Dude Q 74801	Small Town Dude Q 23678
DAM Sorrel Nearly Pretty Q 1015416		Blondy Queen Q 51068
	Pretty Pretty Q 500168	Mr Harlan Q 187419
		Flapper Todd Q 128854

MARKINGS: STAR. SOCKS ON HIND FEET. NO OTHER MARKINGS.

DATE ISSUED   6/13/91

Q2977028

This is to certify that the above named and described horse has been registered with The Palomino Horse Breeders of America, Inc. This certificate is the property of PHBA and is issued in reliance on a written application submitted and attested by the owner, and upon the express condition that the Association has the privilege to correct and/or cancel this certificate for cause under its rules and regulations.

TRANSFER RECORD

...rd is the present owner as indicated in the records of PHBA, INC. To transfer ownership, complete a transfer form ...th this original registration certificate and appropriate fees to PHBA, INC. Transfer entry will then be made on this

SE ONLY — DO NOT WRITE ON THIS CERTIFICATE

...ress of Owner as Shown by Transfer Record | Attest of Record by Secretary

20

Registering Palominos

The Palomino Horse Breeders of America (PHBA) was formed in California in 1941 by a group of horsemen and horsewomen who loved the golden horses. The purpose of the group is to keep track of the **bloodlines** of palomino horses.

To show that a horse meets the requirements for registration with the PHBA, the owner of the horse must complete several forms, pay, and send pictures of the horse. A palomino's owner must have papers showing that one of the horse's parents is a quarter horse, Arabian, American saddlebred, Morgan, or Tennessee walking horse.

One reason owners register horses is because a registered horse is worth more than an unregistered horse. A person buying a registered horse will know what to expect from the horse based on its bloodlines.

The Popular Palomino

Many things have changed since the first palominos came to the New World. The Spanish palominos mixed with many different breeds to produce beautiful palomino horses of many sizes. Today these golden horses can be found throughout the United States and in many other places around the world. There are more than 82,000 horses registered with the Palomino Horse Breeders of America alone.

One thing that has not changed is the beauty of a palomino horse. Whether it is working on a farm, taking part in a horse show, or leading a parade, the palomino always stands out. Horse breeders around the world continue to breed their horses carefully to make sure that palominos will be around for many years to come.

Glossary

bloodlines (BLUD-lynz) An animal's direct blood relatives, such as its parents.

bred (BRED) To have brought a male and a female animal together so they will have babies.

breed (BREED) A group of animals that look alike and have the same relatives.

cremello (kreh-MEL-oh) A light, cream-colored horse.

foals (FOHLZ) Young horses.

legend (LEH-jend) A story, passed down through the years, that cannot be proved.

mares (MERZ) Adult female horses.

recreational (reh-kree-AY-shuh-nul) Having to do with something that is for fun, a hobby.

registered (REH-jih-sterd) Listed officially.

rodeos (ROH-dee-ohz) Sports events in which people's skills in roping cattle and riding horses and bulls are tested against other people's.

saddle (SA-dul) A leather seat that is used on the back of a horse to carry a rider.

stallions (STAL-yunz) Adult male horses.

stock horses (STOK HORS-ez) Workhorses.

withers (WIH-therz) A place between the shoulders of a dog or horse.

Index

A
American saddlebred(s), 5, 18, 21
Arabian(s), 5, 21

B
bloodlines, 21

C
cremello, 10

F
foal(s), 10, 17

I
Isabella, queen of Castile, 5–7

M
mare(s), 6, 10
Morgan(s), 5, 14, 21

N
Native Americans, 5

P
Palomino Horse Association, 10
Palomino Horse Breeders of America (PHBA), 10, 13, 21

Q
quarter horse(s), 5, 14, 21

S
stallion(s), 6, 10

T
Tennessee walking horse(s), 5, 21
Thoroughbreds, 5
Tournament of Roses Parade, 18
training, 17

Web Sites

Due to the changing nature of Internet links, PowerKids Press has developed an online list of Web sites related to the subject of this book. This site is updated regularly. Please use this link to access the list:

www.powerkidslinks.com/horse/palomino/